G000269418

RETRO DINER
Recipes

by Simon Haseltine

*Illustrated with
Nostalgic Diner images
from the American Roadside*

SALMON

The American Diner brings back so many evocative memories of the 1950s, when life was slower, simpler and somehow far more enjoyable. So, if your taste buds yearn for a breakfast bonanza, saucy sandwiches, sizzling steaks, delicious desserts or sparkling sodas, then I hope this collection of recipes helps transport you back a few decades to a time of all-day breakfasts, a noisy juke box, big cars and poodle skirts.

Index

Printed and Published by J. Salmon Ltd., Sevenoaks, England © Copyright

Photographs copyright Ron Saari ©

Delicious Pancakes

6½ oz. plain flour ¾ tsp. salt 2½ tsp. baking powder 2 eggs (beaten)
3 tbsp. white sugar 1 fl.oz. milk 3 tbsp. vegetable oil

Sift together the flour, baking powder, sugar and salt. Mix in the eggs, milk and oil and whisk gently until well mixed. Heat a griddle (or large frying pan) over high heat and add a little oil. Drop spoonfuls of batter on the griddle and cook for a few moments on one side. They are ready to flip when there are little bubbles across the pancake. Flip, cook briefly on the second side and serve with lashings of maple syrup.

Buttermilk Pancakes

12 oz. plain flour 2 tsp. sugar 1 tsp. salt 1 tbsp. baking powder
1 tbsp. baking soda 2 eggs 2 pints buttermilk 2 oz. melted butter

Mix all dry ingredients together and set aside. Next, beat the eggs with buttermilk. Slowly add the dry mix to the wet mix and then stir in the melted butter. Fry each ladle of batter in hot oil and serve with a combination of syrup and lemon juice. Makes around 10 pancakes.

DAVIES'
chuck
wagon

DINER

OPEN

PANCAKES

STEAKS

FRIED CHICKEN

NOW
HIRING

CASHIER

CHUCK WAGON BREAKFAST

STEAK
& EGGS

Waffles

7 oz. plain flour   1 tbsp. white sugar   2 tsp. baking powder   3 eggs
½ tsp. salt   7 tbsp. vegetable oil   14 fl.oz. milk

Preheat the waffle pan or frying pan. Sift the dry ingredients into a bowl. Separate the eggs, reserving the egg whites in a bowl, then beat the egg whites until they are stiff. Next, add the egg yolks, oil and milk to the dry ingredients and beat until there are no lumps in the batter. Fold the egg whites into the batter. Put around ½ cup of batter in the pan to form a 9-inch round waffle and cook until brown both sides. Serve hot with maple syrup. Makes around 8 waffles.

Wonderful Waffles

2 eggs (beaten)   7½ fl.oz. milk   3 tbsp. vegetable oil   6 oz. plain flour
3 tsp. baking powder   2 tsp. sugar   ½ tsp. salt

Mix the eggs and milk in a large bowl, then stir in the flour, baking powder, sugar and salt until well blended. Heat a waffle pan and brush with melted butter or oil. Pour in the batter, close and bake until the steaming stops and waffles are crisp, tender and golden. Makes 4 medium waffles.

Blueberry Yoghurt Pancakes

2½ oz. plain flour	⅛ tsp. nutmeg
1 tbsp. sugar	1 egg (beaten)
1 tsp. baking powder	4 fl.oz. plain yogurt
½ tsp. baking soda	4 fl.oz. milk
¼ tsp. salt	2 tbsp. oil

2 oz. blueberries

In a bowl, sift together the flour, sugar, baking powder, baking soda, salt and nutmeg. In a separate bowl, combine the egg, yogurt and milk. Beat well, then stir in the oil. Next, gradually fold in the flour mixture and combine well, but do not over mix. Pour the mixture using a ladle onto a hot oiled griddle (or frying pan) and drop several blueberries onto each pancake. Flip after bubbles appear on the surface and cook until golden brown. Serve hot with butter and blueberry syrup.

Diner-Style Hash Browns

2½ lbs. potatoes (unpeeled & quartered)
1 small onion (grated)
Salt & freshly ground black pepper, to taste
2 tbsp. unsalted butter
2 tbsp. vegetable oil
2 tbsp. finely-chopped fresh chives or parsley

Place the potatoes in a saucepan with lightly salted cold water and simmer for 5 minutes. Drain well and set aside to cool. Then, grate the cold potatoes over a mixing bowl, add the onion and season with salt and pepper to taste. Place a non-stick griddle over medium heat and melt the butter with the vegetable oil. Form the shredded potato into patties around 1 inch thick and fry for around 5 minutes until the underside is browned and crusty. Using the spatula, turn the hash browns over and continue frying for a further 5 minutes until browned and crusty on the second side. Transfer the potatoes to a warmed serving platter and garnish with chives or parsley. Makes around 6 hash browns.

Apple Cinnamon Muffins

4 small apples (peeled, cored and chopped fine)
2 tbsp. lemon juice   3 eggs   6 fl.oz. vegetable oil
1 tsp. vanilla extract   1½ tsp. baking soda
1½ tsp. salt   1½ tsp. cinnamon
10 oz. plain flour   11 oz. sugar

Preheat oven to 190°C/gas 5. Place the apple pieces into a bowl and toss with the lemon juice. In a separate large bowl, beat the eggs and stir in the sugar, oil and vanilla until well combined. In a small bowl, sift together the dry ingredients: baking soda, salt, cinnamon and flour. Next, add the dry ingredients to the batter and beat gently. Finally, fold the apples pieces into the batter.

In a cupped baking tin with muffin paper liners, dollop the batter evenly and bake for 20 minutes. Remove from the pan and cool on a wire rack. Serves 18.

New England Potato Chowder

8 rashers bacon	2 tbsp. dried parsley
1 medium onion (chopped)	1 tbsp. Worcestershire sauce
3 sticks celery (chopped)	1 tsp. celery salt
1½ oz. plain flour	½ tsp. black pepper
1½ pint single cream	1 large carrot (sliced)
4 medium potatoes (peeled and cubed)	6 green beans (sliced)
2 cans condensed cream of celery soup	1 can sweet corn

In a large pot, fry the bacon until very crispy. Remove and drain on a paper towel and 'crumble' when cool enough to handle. In the bacon fat, sauté the onion and celery for around 5 minutes until tender. Then, sprinkle the flour over the onion mixture and stir until blended. Next, gradually add the cream and fold in the potatoes, soup, parsley and Worcestershire sauce. Season to taste and bring gently to the boil and simmer for a few minutes, stirring all the time. Reduce the heat to a very gentle simmer, cover and cook for a further 25 minutes, stirring occasionally. Next, add the carrots and green beans, cover and simmer for a further 15 minutes or until the vegetables are tender. Finally, stir in the sweet corn and the crumbled bacon. Heat through for a further minute or so and serve. Serves 10.

New Jersey French Toast

7 oz. brown sugar	5 eggs
3½ oz. butter	12 fl.oz. milk
2 tbsp. light corn syrup	1 tsp. vanilla extract
2 tart apples (peeled and sliced)	1 French baguette

Combine the sugar, butter and corn syrup in saucepan. Cook over medium heat until the mixture becomes 'syrupy.' Pour the mixture into a small baking dish and combine with the apple slices. Slice the bread into thin slices and place on top of apple slices. Whisk remaining ingredients together and pour over bread slices. Cover and refrigerate overnight. The following morning, bake, uncovered, at 180°C/gas 4 for 40 minutes or until golden brown and serve for breakfast with a spicy apple syrup.

Club Sandwich

1 tsp. mayonnaise	2 slices turkey breast
2 tsp. sour cream	2 large Romaine lettuce leaves
3-4 tomato slices	2 slices crisp cooked bacon
3 slices whole wheat or white bread, toasted	

First, blend the mayonnaise and sour cream together in a small cup and spread on two of the toasted bread slices. Arrange the turkey breast and 1 leaf of lettuce on one slice of toast. Stack another slice of bread on top of this with the mayonnaise facing up. Then arrange the bacon and remaining lettuce on top of the second slice. Place the tomato slices on top of the lettuce and finally the last piece of bread on top of the sandwich. Cut the sandwich into four triangles, then pierce each triangle with a long toothpick so that all the layers stay together. Makes 1 huge sandwich.

Pulled Pork Sandwiches

3½ lb. (approx) boneless shoulder pork
1 jar apricot jam
7 fl.oz. barbecue sauce

1 large onion (chopped)
2 oz. dried apricots (chopped)
8 baps

Place the pork joint in a slow cooker. In a bowl, combine the jam, barbecue sauce, onion and apricots and pour over the meat. Cook on a low heat setting for 8 hours. Transfer the cooked pork to a cutting board and gently shred (or 'pull'), using 2 large forks. In a large bowl, combine the pulled pork and some of the sauce from the cooker. Place the pulled pork onto sliced baps and top with some of the remaining sauce. Serves 8 with a side dish of coleslaw.

Blue Plate Special

1 lb. minced beef   17½ fl.oz. prepared beef gravy
1 onion (chopped)   4 portions mashed potatoes (hot)

In a large frying pan, brown the beef with the onions for around 5 minutes, draining off any excess liquid. Remove to a bowl and set aside. In the same pan, heat the gravy over medium heat until smooth and slightly thickened. Return the meat to the gravy, mix well and simmer gently for 30 minutes until tender. Serve over the mashed potatoes with peas and carrots on the side. Serves 4.

Diner Salisbury Steak

1 lb. minced beef
2 onions (finely chopped)
2 oz. Italian-seasoned bread crumbs
1 egg

1 tbsp. American yellow mustard.
8½ fl.oz. prepared beef gravy (thick)
2 tsp. prepared white horseradish
7 oz. mushrooms, thinly sliced

In a bowl, combine the minced beef, onions, bread crumbs, egg and mustard, mixing well together. Shape into four ½ inch thick oval patties. Coat a large frying pan with a little oil and heat. Cook the individual patties over a medium heat for around 5 minutes each side, or until cooked through. Add the gravy, horseradish and mushrooms and cook for a further 5 minutes, stirring occasionally. Serve with mashed potato. Serves 4.

Country Fried Steak

8 oz. plain flour
2 tsp. salt
¼ tsp. black pepper
4 (3½ oz.) steaks, trimmed & flattened
2 oz. minced beef

1 oz. plain flour
8½ fl.oz. chicken stock
8½ fl.oz. milk
¼ tsp. black pepper
¼ tsp. salt

Sift the flour (8 oz.), salt and pepper together in a bowl. Dip each steak in water, then into the flour mixture. Bring a deep fat fryer up to 180°C degrees and deep fry each steak in the hot oil for 10 minutes. Drain on paper towels. Next, brown the minced beef in a frying pan for around 5 minutes and stir in the flour (1 oz.) for a further minute. Add the remaining ingredients and bring to boil, then simmer for around 10 minutes until thick. Add the steaks to the minced beef mixture and warm through. Serve with mashed potato. Serves 4.

Diner Meatloaf

1 lb. 10 oz. minced beef	Pinch salt
3½ oz. soft bread crumbs	Pinch pepper
7 fl.oz. milk	Pinch oregano
1 large onion (chopped)	½ tin chopped tomatoes
2 oz. Parmesan cheese	Squeeze tomato puree
1 egg (lightly beaten)	3 slices Mozzarella cheese

Heat oven to 180°C/gas 4. Combine all ingredients except the chopped tomatoes, tomato purée and the Mozzarella cheese. Mix with your fingers until sticky and place in a small greased loaf tin. Bake for 1½ hours, then drain any excess fat. Meanwhile, mix the chopped tomatoes and tomato purée and pour over drained meat loaf. Bake for a further 30 minutes. Finally, layer Mozzarella cheese on top of the meatloaf and return to the oven for a final 10 minutes for the cheese to melt. Serves 6.

Double Decker Hamburgers

1 lb. ground chuck steak   1 large onion (finely chopped)   6 burger buns (halved)
Burger sauce (use shop-bought BBQ sauce or see home-made recipe)   Lettuce, shredded
American cheese (use 8 processed cheese squares)   Pickled gerkins (sliced)

DOUBLE DECKER BURGER SAUCE
1 cup mayonnaise   Splash hot chilli sauce (to taste)   ½ cup tomato ketchup
3 tbsp. sugar   ½ cup pickled gerkins (chopped)   Pinch garlic salt

Mix the minced steak and onions together and divide into 8 equal portions and shape into patties, keeping each quite thin. Sear each burger in a lightly greased hot pan, turning once, until cooked medium-well (or to taste). Arrange each burger on half of the hamburger buns. Add a dollop of BBQ sauce and then arrange a little shredded lettuce over each with the pickled gerkins. Place one atop the other (to form 4 burgers) with 2 slices of American cheese over the top burger. Apply the top burger bun and serve at once. Makes 4 double-burgers.

Crockpot Beef Tips

2½ oz. plain flour	1 can condensed beef broth
1 tsp. salt	1 tsp. Worcestershire sauce
Pinch pepper	2 tsp. ketchup
4 lb. stewing steak	2½ fl.oz. dry red wine
2 onions (chopped)	3 tbsp. plain flour
8 oz. mushrooms (sliced)	

Sift the flour, salt and pepper together and toss in the beef to coat thoroughly. Place beef in crockpot or slow cooker and add the onions and mushrooms. In a medium bowl, combine the broth, Worcestershire sauce and tomato ketchup and pour over beef mixture. Stir well and cook on a low setting for around 10 hours. One hour before serving, turn to High. Make a roux of flour and red wine and stir into the stew. Cover and cook until thickened. Serve over noodles. Serves 10.

Sloppy Joes

1 lb. 2 oz. minced ground beef	2 tbsp. brown sugar
1 medium onion (chopped)	2 tsp. Worcestershire sauce
One small can crushed pineapple	¼ tsp. dry mustard
One large can chopped tomato	¼ tsp. salt
2 tbsp. white vinegar	1 French baguette

Brown the minced beef and the onion in a frying pan for around 5 minutes. Then add the undrained pineapple, chopped tomatoes (but reserve a little juice), vinegar, brown sugar, Worcestershire sauce, mustard and salt. Simmer, uncovered for around 20 minutes or until the sauce thickens, adding the remaining tomato juice if required.

Meanwhile, cut the baguette into 4 inch chunks, halve and toast the non-crust side. Spoon the beef mixture generously over the toasted baguettes for a delicious and messy lunch.

Philadelphian Cheese Steak and Onion Sandwiches

2 large onions (thinly sliced)   3 tsp. olive oil   1 lb. 2 oz. boneless top sirloin steak
Salt and pepper   4 6-inch sub rolls, split partially open lengthwise
4 slices American cheese (use processed square cheese slices)

Heat a little olive oil in a large frying pan over medium-high heat. Add the onions and cook for around 5 minutes until softened. Remove them from the pan and set aside but keep warm. Meanwhile, cut the steak into bite-size chunks and place between 2 films of clingfilm. Using a meat mallet, flatten the cubes until paper thin. Sprinkle with salt and pepper. Sauté the steak in the remaining oil quickly over a high heat and then remove from the pan. Divide the steak between the sub rolls and top with the onions and a slice of cheese. Grill for 2 minutes or until the cheese melts. Serves 4.

Cincinnati Chilli

1 lb. 2 oz. minced beef	1 tsp. cumin
1 large onion (chopped)	½ tsp. cayenne
1 clove garlic (crushed)	½ tsp. salt
1 tbsp. olive oil	1 tbsp. cocoa powder
1 tbsp. chilli powder	1 can chopped tomatoes
1 tsp. allspice	1 tbsp. Worcestershire sauce
1 tsp. cinnamon	1 tbsp. cider vinegar

Sauté the minced beef, onion and garlic in large frying pan until browned. Add all the remaining ingredients and simmer for around 30 to 40 minutes until the sauce has thickened. Serve over a 'Twice Baked Potato'. Serves 4.

Fishwich
With Home-made American Tartar Sauce

1 lb. cod fillets   Black pepper, to taste   4 Burger buns   Sweet pickle relish
Mayonnaise   Pinch paprika   4 slices American cheese (square processed cheese)

Fry the cod at 180°C/gas 4. in a deep fat fryer for about 3 minutes, or until lightly browned. Drain well in the basket then on kitchen paper towels afterwards. Next, prepare the tartar sauce by mixing the pepper, sweet pickle relish, mayonnaise and paprika together in a small bowl. Finally, place a cooked fish portion on bottom half of a burger bun. Add 1 slice cheese, then a dollop of your home-made tartar sauce on top. Add the top half bun to make sandwich and serve immediately. Serves 4.

American Diner Fries

5 large baking potatoes
Fresh frying oil (enough to fill your deep fat fryer)
Salt

Wash and peel the potatoes, trim into even rectangles and cut into lengthwise slices around ⅜ inch wide, then rinse in cold water. Pat dry before frying.

The first fry: Heat the oil to 160°C/gas 2. Take 2 handfuls of dry potato chips and place into the frying basket. Lower into the hot fat and fry for around 5 minutes, or until the potatoes are soft through but not yet browned. Lift out the basket, let it drain briefly, then spread the potatoes on a paper towel and continue frying remaining potatoes. Let cool for at least 10 minutes.

The second frying: Just before serving, heat the frying oil to 190°C/gas 5. Fry the cooked potatoes by handfuls, as before, turning frequently, for 2 minutes or until golden brown. Drain on paper towels and salt lightly. Serve with any diner dish for a true American experience. Makes 6 servings.

Old-Fashioned Diner Onion Rings

4 large onions (thickly sliced to form rings)   2 eggs
7 oz. plain flour   5 oz. dry bread crumbs   2 tsp. baking powder
Garlic powder (to taste)   2 tsp. salt   Oil for frying
Around ½ pint of milk (adjust to form a thick batter)

Heat the oil in a deep-fryer to 180°C/gas 4. Separate the onion slices into rings and set aside. In a small bowl, stir together the flour, baking powder, salt and garlic powder. Dip the onion slices into the flour mixture until they are all coated. Next, whisk the egg and milk into the remaining flour mixture using a fork to form a thick batter. Dip the floured rings into the batter to coat, then place on a wire rack to drain. Now place the battered onion rings (one at a time) into a bowl of bread crumbs and scoop the crumbs up over the ring to coat evenly. Deep fry the rings a few at a time for 2 to 3 minutes, or until golden brown. Remove to paper towels to drain. Season with garlic salt and serve hot. Serves 6.

Boston Baked Beans

2 lb. navy pea beans   4 oz. dark brown sugar   2 tsp. dry mustard
4½ oz. molasses (dark brown)   7 oz. smoked cooked gammon (finely chopped)
2 onions (chopped)   Salt

Rinse the beans thoroughly in cold water, strain and place in a large saucepan and cover with fresh cold water. Soak overnight. In the morning, add 1 tsp. of salt and simmer for 1 hour, skimming off the foam. Drain, but save the liquid.

Preheat oven to 150°C/gas 3. Add beans to a casserole dish, together with the sugar, mustard, molasses, onions, gammon and the reserved liquid. Bake the beans in the middle of the oven for about 7 hours. Check halfway through and add a little extra water if necessary. Serve at supper time that evening.

Home-on-the-Range Ranch Dressing

5 fl.oz. sour cream   1 clove garlic (crushed)   2½ fl.oz. mayonnaise
1 tsp. black pepper   Pinch salt   1 tbsp. water   2 tsp. white vinegar

In a small bowl, beat together the sour cream, mayonnaise, salt, vinegar, black pepper and water. Stir the crushed garlic into the dressing and thin out with a little more water if required. Cool and drizzle over a salad.

Highway Coleslaw

1 small white cabbage (shredded)   2 carrots (grated)   1 small red cabbage (shredded)
1 large onion (grated)   4 tbsp. fresh parsley (shredded)   2 tsp. salt
Pinch white pepper   ¼ pint single light cream   14 fl.oz. mayonnaise
2½ fl.oz. apple cider vinegar   1 tsp. celery seed

Mix together the shredded cabbage, carrot and onion and chill for 30 minutes. Mix together the remaining ingredients, then pour over cabbage mixture and fold in to blend ingredients. Chill overnight and serve with a Summer Caesar Salad.

Strawberry Pie

½ pint water

5 oz. white sugar

Pinch salt

2 tbsp. cornflour

¼ tsp. red food colouring

4 oz. plain flour

4 oz. margarine

3 tbsp. confectioner's sugar

1 tsp. vanilla extract

2 large handfuls fresh strawberries (hulled)

1 packet/tub dessert topping (whipped)

Mix together the water, white sugar, salt, cornflour and food colouring and cook in a saucepan for about 5 minutes or until thickened. Set aside to cool. Make the crust by combining flour, margarine, confectioner's sugar and vanilla to form a dough, then line a greased 9-inch pie pan. Prick all over and bake blind at 180°C/gas 4 until lightly browned. When the crust is cool, place the strawberries in the shell and pour the thickened mixture over the top. Refrigerate until set. Serves 4 with a dollop of whipped dessert topping.

Hot Fudge Dessert

1 tub vanilla ice cream   Hot fudge sauce (recipe follows)
Whipped cream   4 maraschino cherries   Chopped nuts

Place 2 scoops of vanilla ice cream into each sundae dish. Pour the hot fudge sauce over ice cream and top with whipped cream. Finally, add a maraschino cherry and sprinkle with chopped nuts. Serves 4.

Quick Hot Fudge Sauce

½ cup unsweetened cocoa powder   ½ cup white sugar
⅓ cup corn syrup (use golden syrup if not available)   ½ cup evaporated milk
1 tbsp. sour cream   4 tbsp. unsalted butter   1 tsp. vanilla extract

Combine the cocoa, corn syrup, milk and sour cream in a heavy saucepan. Heat over medium heat, stirring constantly, until the mixture begins to boil. Remove from the heat immediately and then stir in the butter and vanilla extract. Serve warm over ice cream sundae. Serves 4 hot fudge sundaes.

Route 66 Brownies

8 oz. butter (softened)	1 lb. cocoa powder
13 oz. white sugar	4½ oz. plain flour
3 eggs (beaten)	2 oz. white chocolate chips
1 tsp. vanilla essence	2 oz. milk chocolate chips

Preheat oven to 180°C/gas 4 and grease a 9 x12 inch rectangular baking dish. Next, beat the butter until very smooth, then beat in the sugar and mix well. Add the eggs, a little at a time, and beat until smooth. Sift together the cocoa and flour and add to the butter mixture with vanilla essence and mix by hand. Spread into prepared baking tray and sprinkle the chocolate chips over the top of the mixture. Bake for 30–45 minutes until cooked.

Butterscotch Meringue Pie

PIE

Pie crust for a 9-inch pie dish   6½ oz. brown sugar   2½ oz. plain flour   Pinch salt
17½ fl.oz. milk   3 egg yolks   2 tbsp. butter   ½ tsp. vanilla

MERINGUE TOPPING

3 egg whites   ¼ tsp. cream of tartar   3 tbsp. sugar   ½ tsp. vanilla

Prepare the base by layering the crust in the pie plate and pleat the edges.

In a glass bowl combine the brown sugar, flour, salt, and milk. Gently heat over a pan of boiling water (but not touching the water) until the mixture thickens, stirring all the time, then remove from the heat. Add 3 egg yolks, stirring in one at a time, then add the butter and vanilla, mixing well. Pour into the prepared crust. Bake at 180°C/gas 4 for 40 minutes, or until set. Remove from oven and allow to cool on a wire rack while you prepare the meringue.

Pre-chill a bowl in the fridge and add the 3 egg whites with the cream of tartar. Beat the egg whites until soft and forming peaks. Next, gradually add the sugar and continue to beat until stiff but not dry. Finally, fold in vanilla. Dollop the meringue over the cooling pie and spread across the surface and use a spoon to give the meringue peaks. Return the pie to the oven at 180°C/gas 4 for 8–10 minutes until the peaks of the meringue are golden brown. Remove from oven and allow to cool.   Serves 8 slices.

Blueberry Cheesecake

BASE
5 oz. digestive biscuit crumbs   2 oz. brown sugar
3 oz. butter   1 tsp. cinnamon

FILLING
4 x 250g. packages cream cheese, softened   6½ oz. sugar
2 tsp. lemon juice   1 tsp. vanilla extract   4 eggs

Preheat oven to 150°C/gas 3. Lightly grease a 9-inch spring-form flan dish.

To make the crust, combine biscuit crumbs, sugar, and cinnamon in a bowl. Melt the butter and pour over the crumbs and mix well with a fork. Press into the bottom of the flan dish.

For the filling, beat the cream cheese until smooth in a large bowl, then add the sugar and continue beating until well blended. Add the lemon juice, vanilla extract and one egg and mix. Add the remaining eggs, one at a time, beating until the batter is smooth.

Pour the filling into the crust and bake in the centre of the oven for 1 hour 15 minutes, or until set. Cool on wire rack, then chill in the fridge. Serve garnished with a dollop of cream and fresh blueberries.

Peanut Butter Chocolate Chunk Pie

1 lb. pack soft cream cheese   4 oz. smooth peanut butter   3 oz. icing sugar
½ tsp. vanilla   8 fl.oz. whipping cream   7 oz. dark chocolate (chopped)
18 inch prepared biscuit base (using chocolate digestives)
2 oz. dark chocolate (melted)

In small bowl, beat together the cream cheese and peanut butter until light and fluffy. Add the icing sugar and vanilla and continue to mix for a further minute. Fold in the chopped chocolate pieces. In large bowl, beat whipping cream until stiff peaks form. Fold the cream cheese mixture into whipped cream and then spoon over crust. Finally, drizzle the melted chocolate over the cheese cake and chill for 2 hours before serving. Makes 8 servings.

Caramel Sauce

30 caramel chocolate squares   2 fl.oz. water

Melt the caramel squares and water together in a bowl over hot but not boiling water, stirring occasionally. Serve warm over vanilla ice cream.

Strawberry Sauce

1 lb. fresh strawberries   4 oz. granulated sugar   2 fl.oz. orange juice
Finely grated zest of ½ lemon   2 tbsp. butter

Hull and slice the strawberries. In a saucepan, combine sugar and orange juice. Bring to a light boil, then add the lemon zest and strawberries. Heat through for a moment and stir in the butter. Remove from heat and let cool. Chill for serving over strawberry ice cream.

Butterscotch Sauce

6 oz. light brown sugar   2 oz. single cream   2 tbsp. butter
2 tbsp. light corn syrup (or golden syrup)

Combine all ingredients in a heavy saucepan. Bring to a boil over medium heat, stirring occasionally for a minute. Serve hot over vanilla ice cream.

Chocolate Ice Cream

4 oz. icing sugar	17½ fl.oz. milk
4 egg yolks	2 oz. cocoa powder
1 tsp. cornflour	

Gently bring the milk to the boil in a heavy-based saucepan. At the same time, whisk together the sugar, cornflour and egg yolks. Mix the cocoa powder with the milk (following packet instructions if some pre-mixing required) and slowly pour the hot chocolate into the egg mixture while continuing to beat it. Bring back to a simmer and continue stirring until the mixture thickens. Let the mixture chill completely and then freeze in an ice cream maker, in accordance with the maker's instructions.

Traditional American Apple Pie

Short crust pastry (using 255g. flour)
6 medium Granny Smith apples
9 oz. sugar
1½ oz. plain flour

2 tbsp. butter
1 tsp. cinnamon
Pinch nutmeg
A little milk and extra sugar for top crust

Preheat the oven to 220°C/gas 7. Roll out and place one third of the pastry on a pie plate and prick the bottom with a fork. Peel and core apples and slice thickly (say, six slices per apple) and place on the crust. Mix the sugar and flour and sprinkle over the apples. Dot the butter over the apples and finish with a dusting of cinnamon and nutmeg. Roll and lay the top crust over the pie and crimp the edges. Brush the crust with milk and sprinkle with sugar. Cut a single central vent hole, cover loosely with foil and place in the oven.

Cook at 220°C/gas 7 in oven for 10 minutes, then reduce heat to 190°C/gas 5 and cook for a further 45 minutes, removing the foil for the last 10 minutes of baking. Cool slightly on wire rack and serve with a scoop (or two!) of vanilla ice cream.

Root Beer Float

4 scoops vanilla ice cream   16 oz. bottle root beer

Pour the chilled root beer to fill half of each glass. Carefully add one scoop of ice cream to each glass, then slowly fill the glass with the remaining root beer. Serves 4.

Cherry Coke

1 pkg cherry-flavoured Kool-Aid   12 fl.oz. water
3½ oz. granulated sugar   Tins of coke (ice cold)

Stir together all the Kool-Aid, water and sugar until well mixed and refrigerated. To make a glass of ice cold cherry coke, add 3 tablespoons to each glass of coke.

ALTERNATIVES: For a vanilla coke, add ½ tbsp. vanilla extract.
For a chocolate coke, add chocolate syrup to taste.

Chocolate Shake

4 Scoops vanilla ice cream   12 fl.oz. milk (cold)
4 tbsp. chocolate syrup   1 tsp. vanilla extract

Combine all the ingredients in a blender container and blend until smooth. Divide into 4 glasses and serve immediately.

Malts

2–3 scoops vanilla ice cream   7 fl.oz. milk (cold)   2 heaping tbsp. malted milk powder

In a blender or old-fashioned malt mixer (or use a measuring jug and a potato masher), combine and blend all the ingredients until thick and smooth. Add more ice cream to make it thicker if you wish. Serves 1.

ALTERNATIVES:

CHOCOLATE MALT: Use chocolate ice cream.

BANANA SPLIT MALT: Add chocolate syrup, ½ banana, strawberries, pineapple and a cherry on top before you serve.

PEANUT BUTTER CHOCOLATE MALT: Chop up a peanut butter cup candy bar and mix into the basic malt. Add chocolate syrup to serve.

SANTA'S MALT: Use peppermint ice cream and add some mini chocolate chips. Sprinkle with red and green M&Ms on top and serve.

AFTER DINNER MINTY MALT: Use mint chocolate chip ice cream. Crush some chocolate-covered mint chocolates and mix into the malt with a spoon.

METRIC CONVERSIONS

The weights, measures and oven temperatures used in the preceding recipes can be easily converted to their metric equivalents. The conversions listed below are only approximate, having been rounded up or down as may be appropriate.

Weights

Avoirdupois	Metric
1 oz.	just under 30 grams
4 oz. (¼ lb.)	app. 115 grams
8 oz. (½ lb.)	app. 230 grams
1 lb.	454 grams

Liquid Measures

Imperial	Metric
1 tablespoon (liquid only)	20 millilitres
1 fl. oz.	app. 30 millilitres
1 gill (¼ pt.)	app. 145 millilitres
½ pt.	app. 285 millilitres
1 pt.	app. 570 millilitres
1 qt.	app. 1.140 litres

Oven Temperatures

	°Fahrenheit	Gas Mark	°Celsius
Slow	300	2	150
	325	3	170
Moderate	350	4	180
	375	5	190
	400	6	200
Hot	425	7	220
	450	8	230
	475	9	240

Flour as specified in these recipes refers to plain flour unless otherwise described.